Out of the Mouth
of Shame

Out of the Mouth of Shame

Tahtianna Alston

Out of the Mouth of Shame

Copyright © 2020 by Tahtianna Alston

ISBN: 978-1-7354370-0-2
Library of Congress Control Number: 2020913748

Dedication

This book is dedicated to those who are on a journey to become better than they were yesterday, last night, last month, or last year. It is not too late, and you have not done too much to be restored. There is still hope.

Table of Contents

Introduction

I am not sure how to write this book, but this is how I will begin. Today, I am closer to where I want to be, yet the journey has not ceased. I have found myself going in circles year after year, searching for identity and purpose – attempting to find myself in people and things.

During this time, I was the epitome of someone with itching ears, just waiting to get a word or confirmation. When I sought answers from many people, I was often left with a void, or feeling of emptiness. I felt less satisfied than before I had asked questions. They would give an answer that I was already aware of or simply did not want to hear. I was searching for a deeper experience. However, this did not put a block in my efforts to seek answers from others. Wasting my time and theirs, I knew I already had the answers.

There have been challenges in trying to select the best path, which I hoped would lead to joy, happiness and success. Not because the decision was difficult to make, but because the lens in which I saw myself did not align with the words that my heavenly father had spoken over my life. Being engulfed in the knowingness of being strange, I attempted to mold myself into a shape that could be forced into a box, forced into a place I would never fit in. There was a time when I did not see myself as valuable. For some strange reason, people would gravitate towards me but would not stay. Was there something wrong with me? There may have been, as I repelled whoever got too close to me. I was afraid to be myself, knowing I was strange and intelligent. Some may say 'you're trippin." Truth is, my experience revealed that many, especially boys and men, were intimidated by my intelligence. Seems that I could not simultaneously be beautiful and smart.

There was also a battle in my mind with low self-esteem and depression. I developed a lifestyle of trying to please others, that I compromised my health, integrity, values and morals. Though not completely successful in my efforts, steps have been made to break these unhealthy habits. It has taken me years to learn to love myself the way I want to be loved. Though not completely where I want to be, it is progress.

Ten years ago, I would not have imagined that I would be in this space, with these issues on my mind. I miss my younger self. Though I had normal childhood experiences of what I thought of myself, it never stopped me from doing what I wanted to do, what I had dreamed of doing. As an adult, I have visions and dreams, and I feel stuck – paralyzed with fear because there are some things that are supposed to come with getting older, but should letting your dreams die be one of them? The idea of getting older just to work and pay bills crushes me. I cannot believe this is the reality that I have succumbed to.

"Sometime I still doubt myself, but at least now I love myself. And I am quite emotional, that's why you can't get close at all. So, I start to push away the ones that love me cause I'm scared that they might walk away. I'm not perfect, so I try everyday and I grow a little bit," (Cleo Sol, *Why Don't You*).

Someday, the things that held me bound will not be a distant memory, but a testimony of how I became free. Sharing my truth will aid with that, as I choose to come out of hiding and expose the lies I have been holding onto. The time is now. I hope that whoever reads this can grow with me also. It is by faith that I believe you will leave with hope, healing, freedom, or a renewed sense of self.

To those reading my words, thank you for joining me on the journey to heal. I am thankful for your healing as well and pray for your protection as you shed your old and embrace your new.

Guide me
Guide me to the free me
The one who speaks freely
Shouting over the mountain tops me.
Lead me with a hand of certainty
with a force that pushes those that hurt me
protection from those who don't deserve me.
The self-assured me.
Take me to a place of no fear,
of abundance
Not bound in my mind
It's freedom time!

To the girl that has been talked about
whose hair is so different -
whose body may curve or be slim fit
Embrace it
You are wonderfully made
It is your moment
No more shame. No more fear.
This is you
So I am me

Good Morning

My life was once poetry. Mornings held peace, as nature and I conversed, parting the darkness and welcoming the morning light. Having much favor, I encountered no delays during my morning travel to school. This was the time when many individuals were still asleep, so I was able to enjoy myself a bit. My walk was intentional. My hips gently swayed from side to side, with purpose, my feet placed itself on the ground one step after another, the birds whistled, the breeze whispered, my words, fluid. I had a thought and it was not long before it would manifest.

I felt good. I was poetry. We were in sync, nature and me. This was God's work. I sought after God at the age of 14 and accepted him into my heart, so I thought. The oneness I had experienced derived from my new relationship with Him. I felt a flood of love rush over me, covering me. I woke up from my sleep in a blanket of peace, smiling. I had never experienced this before. This was not like the love depicted on television where it was full of lust, and they wanted to tear each other's clothes off. This was genuine love! Being saved was great, and all I had to do was go up to the altar and believe in my heart that Jesus died for my sins and rose from the dead on the third day. I later learned that this is just one step in being transformed in Christ.

Relationships take work. It is one thing to simply enter into a covenant, and another to maintain what has been started amongst involved parties. At fourteen, I did not think of this new lifestyle as something I had to continually work towards. It was honestly my belief that going to the altar was it, in addition to waiting for marriage to have sex. Was there any expectation at all, besides hoping to be the next Virgin Mary? There was not. Little did I know that this new lifestyle would bring many tests. This, I was not prepared for.

I was a baby in Christ and did not know which way to go after being saved. This was a path I was not completely educated on. I knew about Noah and the Ark, Jonah and the big fish, Moses parting the Red Sea, and being "blessed and highly favored"; but I did not know much more than the popular bible stories, sayings, and scriptures. I thought getting saved was the end all be all, and there was nothing else I needed to do besides do my best to live right, whatever that looked like. Boy was I wrong. My ignorance was the beginning of a downward spiral, where I wish I had someone to guide me during this time, especially as a young lady.

See me as I am, not as I am not
Do not pick away at my petals because you do not like the
flower that I am
Nor paint me a different shade because you do no like the
color of my aura.
I am a picture bigger than the frame that fits me.

The Planting

A flower is delicate. It has a beauty of its very own. Before it is a flower, it is a seed. The seed is planted into a bed of already prepared soil, in which the best spot has been selected for well required growth. The seed is watered and is now ready to begin its journey. Some planters like to talk to their seeds, speaking positive words encouraging it to grow. You notice that it does not take effect immediately, but later see what is coming to be. Your seed is no longer a seed, but a sprout, then something bigger. Its tiny petals conceal what is safely being kept on the inside. Though it is not yet revealed, the full flower, it is still cared for. Stormy weather and outside factors hit the growing specimen. It does not fall but becomes strong due to the hardship it has endured and the care that was given to it.

The day has come where the flower has opened its petals and showed off its beauty to the world. The great arrival has come and there is still maintenance work to be done. Would the outcome have been different if all of the steps were not completed? You never know how the outcome is affected until you realize and understand the contribution of a missing factor.

I am the only girl and the oldest of my mother's four children. Three of us grew up in a single parent household and still managed to do pretty well in school. Outside of school was a different story. Being a young, single parent is no easy task. Yet my mother has done a good job rearing us.

At home, my brothers and I would play around the house, creating such a big mess. We used anything we could find as our toys; these days were fun while they lasted. As we grew old enough to take responsibility for ourselves, my mother took on more hours at work in order to take care of the household (bills, food, children, our school needs, etc.). I carried on the responsibility of fixing meals for my brothers and me. I also had to establish some sort of discipline for when they would get too out of hand or just would not do as I asked them to, such as clean the mess that they had made.

Mom would come home early in the morning from work and we would all go to a restaurant for breakfast. We would then see her for the majority of the day until the evening would come and she would be off to work again. This was our daily routine. I began to miss my mother. I did not always want to be the responsible one. I was about eleven or twelve years old at the time. I wanted to enjoy some childhood activities also. Though I was involved in afterschool activities and programs, I did not want that good feeling to last only when I was at school. Afterschool, not only was I a sister-mom, but I had to manage getting my homework done while maintaining the home as well. In this reflection, I recall some of the sacrifices that were made for me to experience other activities.

I remember being in the Young Scholars program when my family and I had become homeless. She tried to avoid making the decision to go to a shelter, my mom. In the end, that is where we ended up going. At the shelter, if you were not signed in by a certain time, you were at risk of losing your bed for the night. My mom took the risk of taking me to my mandatory Young Scholars meeting, during the time we were supposed to check-in for the night. She let someone know in advance, but technically, our spot was not to be held. There were moments when my mom also stayed outside and waited for me when I wanted to participate in school dances or events. She no longer had a vehicle after getting into an accident, at no fault of her own. I know because she was taking me to school that morning. I was selfish in my thinking as an adolescent. Yes, it seemed like everyone was having fun with friends but me, but I did not want to experience it like that. I was embarrassed because we didn't have it like that, but my mama and brothers would wait on me at the end of each event I attended.

Thank you for your sacrifice mom.

After we got a home and became more settled, things started changing again. One of my brothers had reached an age where he could begin to take on responsibility while I did more things after school. I learned to get around the city on my own, by this time. I was in the school choir seventh and eighth grade year. During my eighth grade year, I took on playing the drums, singing in the choir, and joined the dance team. I loved it all. It was something that came naturally to me.

Without the full responsibility of having to watch my brothers all the time, I began to occupy my mind elsewhere. Boys became an interest to me, in which I could never give much attention to before. Growing older, I would notice that I would engage in a relationship with a boy, even if he did not meet my full standards or I did not necessarily like him. I never walked up to a boy and told them that I liked them. Instead, they would come up to me, or write a note that says "circle yes or no if you like me." I often circled "yes" because I thought the idea was cute, I thought they actually liked me, or I did not want to hurt their feelings by rejecting them. I noticed, in the end, that all I wanted was for someone to care for me and tell me that they love me. This was not always apparent to my developing mind.

Unconsciously searching for love and acceptance did not lead me towards the places I needed to be. I became desperate for the feeling without taking notice of it. I wanted so bad to have a loving relationship with someone. I wanted to know that I was relevant and that I was important to someone besides my mother. Why was this becoming a thing with me? Why did I want so badly to get this feeling that I was apparently yearning for? The feeling of loneliness waded inside of me, reflecting something important that I lacked. I didn't have a clue of what this feeling was.

I was once a seed, planted by both my mother and father. After the planting of the seed, my father left and did not put any love into my growth. My mother was the planter who spoke encouraging words and was patient with me, even when results did not show as quickly as she would have liked them to. I am a flower, but in the process of my growing period, I was missing a very important factor for my growth, my father. Yet, I stand. This flower has been dragged through the dirt and at times has had to have tape placed on the stem to keep it up and sturdy. Does that not make me a flower? Am I now a weed because I have been tainted by societal influences? No. I may not be the same flower as many, but I am still a flower. Not having my father has made me feel unlovable, in the past, simply because he was not there to show me that I was. My heart felt unbalanced.

I used to look at myself in the mirror and tried to figure out what my dad looked like. What features of his resided in me? I was really excited to know. People always said that I look like my mother, but my mother would always tell me that I look like my dad. My fingers, she said, are piano fingers, like my dad's. My toes, they are long and narrow just like his. A piece of my personality reminds my mother of him. Listening to these similarities often made me so curious to what else we had in common. I then began to wonder why he wasn't here with us.

'How come we could not be like a real family with two parents"? This question did not begin until events like the father-daughter dance occurred in school. All of the students would talk about how fun their fathers are and what they would wear. When it came to me, I had nothing to say. I began to feel very sad and left out. Why don't I have a father? Why can't I have two parents ? It was often said while I was growing up that having a father in a child's life was important. Though I felt sad at times that he was not there, I thought my mom did a pretty good job rearing my brothers and me. People would always compliment her on how well behaved we were and how intelligent we were. Overall, I believe that she deserves an award for taking care of her children on her own and doing such a good job of it.

Fast Track

It was the summer before I began my freshman year of high school when I became a member of a local percussion group. I played drums in middle school and was very excited when the opportunity came to me. The group was composed of a majority of males and three females including myself. After being pursued by one of the members, it was not long before I opened myself to the opportunity.

It seemed like in that same hour is when I had lost my virginity – not because I wanted to, but because I felt I was supposed to. I remember the guy trying to convince me of how grown I was. He was older than me, with his own apartment and his own car. He was also involved with music, which is where I got my first beat making program, Fruity Loops 7. He turned on some music when we drove around in his car. It had an effect on me. He produced his own music! Creating music and putting lyrics to match was something I have wanted to do for a few years. I told him I wanted to make my own music. That's when he gave me his fully purchased program. I had access to everything I needed.

He brought us back to his apartment and showed me around. There was not much to see. I just remember it being filled with the bare minimum: a couch, a T.V., and bare, white walls. He called me to his room and said, 'Sit on my lap". I told him I was scared. He laughed a little and guided me by the hand, told me to relax, and it happened. What was the big deal? I did not feel anything great about the moment. He was happy, so I pretended to be happy. For the next few days, I was bleeding. He called it, 'popping my cherry." I had no idea what this meant, but I rolled with it. I was so invested in the cherry, that I bought cherry everything – cherry Clear Fruit, cherry lollipops, cherry cherries, you name it.

When I think about it today, I do not know why a grown man would be so excited about taking the virginity of a young girl, but who was going to stop it? Not me.

Womanhood:

> *My panties grew in size overnight.*
> *I was now able to do grown woman things.*

Grooming

He often told me how cute I was and gawked at the idea that I could be his sugar baby. He was in his 20s, I believe 23 or 25. I initially thought he was a teenager. He was a short man, with braids, and one or two gold pieces in his mouth. He showed me his removable grills. I liked his teeth better without them. Either way it went, I liked him and he did nothing wrong to me.

The more I was with him, the more he became the center of my world. He knew about the problems I thought I had at home and my life at school. So, his age did not matter because there was already a relationship established. I had an idea of what a sugar daddy was, but had no clue of what he was talking about as it related to me. Later that day, we had gone to the mall and went into Victoria Secret. I bought my own panties to show how grown I was. Thinking of it now, I do not believe he offered to pay. I was trying to make an impression, but I wanted to be frugal. Luckily for me, there was a 5 for $25 deal. The panties looked basic to me, just varied in color and trim.

It was not long before I felt the after effects of what I had allowed to happen. As a surprise to me, I was the one left with the impression. After our first encounter, I craved sex daily, though I did not care much for my first experience. If someone would have asked me how this happened, I would not be able to give an answer. I would stare out the window at school, planning the quickest route to my desired destination. It was like an annoying itch that I could not scratch. I was hooked and could not shake it. I felt like an addict and thought I would go crazy if I did not satisfy the crave. This was new for me and I was confused on who to talk to about this. The only other person I considered talking to was a close friend, and she was having sex as well. I was excited that we were on the same journey again. For a second, I was starting to feel like I was getting left behind. She lost her virginity before me. I was not too pressed, but we were beginning to run out of things to talk about, as if she had outgrown me. I did not want to lose my friend.

The stories she told me were interesting, as she shared some of the things that she did. I soaked up the information like a sponge. It was also easy to pick up ideas from the songs that were out. That is all everyone really talked about, sex. After the years of empowerment to the young people had gone away, a wave of prostitution to the minds and bodies of the young people took over.

The thrill of sex was but a vapor. There was a particular day where he had gone to the store and left me in his apartment. I took this opportunity to look through a few movies for him and I to watch when he returned. What I found was a home video of him having sex with a girl. "Is that me?" I asked myself. Our complexion was about the same, as well as the size of the body. As I continued to look at her back, the difference was found in the booty. It wasn't me. I believed the video was before he and I got together, but why did he still have it, and how old was it?

It didn't take long to notice other red flags. It was later discovered that he had a son. In the distance there was a girl leaving his place as I was making my way there after school. I turned around without hesitation – did not care what the reason was or who she was. That was it, and we have not seen one another, or talked since.

I physically left him. The addiction was still there.

Little girl, little girl.
Your mind has been warped into a black hole
which you cannot seem to escape from.
Your body and mind severed.
Your soul, lost and not found.
You are wandering in the dark.

Is a Rose Still a Rose?

What kind of woman am I? One who is overly emotional and can't get my head on straight; or one who is quiet and lets people run over her? Maybe both. From being bitter, to getting my Jazmine Sullivan on, to entertaining someone else's man with my words and thoughts of what could be. I had changed. I was entertaining an old love that never moved past the puppy dog stage.

The relationship was brief but it had a lasting impact on me. He was someone that truly cared about me back then, and I never forgot the feelings entangled with it all. He did not drop my hand when other women came around, he held it up high. He was one to genuinely love my hair in its natural state, unlike when I was told that I could be in a slave movie because of it, or when I was compared to Aunt Jemima when I wore my scarf at night. I selfishly wanted to be loved with a pure-like heart again, by him. Even if all he wanted was sex, I could not tell because I was blinded by the small things he formerly did. He looked into my eyes when we talked to one another, and allowed space to be filled by pulsing hearts and cool breezes.

After running in circles in some of the most damaging relationships I have been involved in, I was searching for an escape. It took me two days, after reminiscing and entertaining possibilities, to see that I was undeniably wrong. I was not his woman and he was not my man. I have developed ways of a woman, a person, whom I never wanted to be – operating in selfishness. I am ashamed. I am ashamed of what I have become. I could wonder how I really got here, but there is really no excuse for my actions.

I moved in the area of hurt because I was hurt. Hardly ever did I care about how it would impact those around me until the act was already done. After each occurrence, I would feel guilt, yet I continued to do what I would do. This was my new lifestyle and I did not know how to get out of it. Not many knew, but I was cold and bitter inside. That is where all of my secrets stayed, inside, where I drowned in silence.

My mama did not rear me to be this way and I never envisioned this for my life. What I envisioned was an intelligent young girl blossoming into a beautiful woman, fearless of whatever stood before her. I saw a woman who made her mother proud. One who stood tall in grace and walked in humbleness. I saw beauty.

My mama was always busy with work. When I would go through things, I did not know who to talk to because I was the oldest, and it was my responsibility to take care of the boys while she worked. I sometimes wanted to open up to my brothers, but how would they look at me? Would they think I am gross? Maybe so. Besides, I would never want to put a burden on them that is not theirs to worry about or carry. I am the oldest. The only outlet I had as a child was dancing, writing and music. I wrote music often and danced daily. It was my medicine and kept me in times when I did not feel so well.

Other times I came across stories on the internet, of individuals who killed themselves, for various reasons. I wanted to kill myself at times too, but I could not. It does not mean I did not try; I just was not successful in my attempts. I was too afraid to try anything drastic and painful. As I think of these moments, I cannot strongly recall why I wanted to end my own life, but I do remember how lonely I felt as a little girl. I was depressed and had occasional, recurring bouts of sadness. In my sadness, I would cry in silence and eat through my emotions, which eventually led to binge eating, which led to attempts in starving myself because I felt the guilt of how much I ate in a small span of time – then I would do it all over again. This became an additional cycle, an illness. This was all before the age of 11, and no one but myself, knew this was happening.

"Binge eating involves consuming large quantities of food very quickly, even when not hungry, and to the point of being uncomfortable. Almost everyone overeats once in a while, but it can also become a disorder," (Jennifer R. Scott, "What is Binge Eating", June 4, 2020). " "Many factors play into the formation of an eating disorder, including an individual's family history or situation, genetics, and cultural standards. However, people with a history of depression, anxiety, or obsessive-compulsive behaviors are often at higher risk for developing an eating disorder," (Samantha Gluck, "Eating Disorders: Common in Young Girls").

It may seem like it would be obvious if someone is an overeater, but I was naturally a small girl. My grades were very good, I exercised and I did not display any unordinary behaviors. I also did not look underweight. With the information being accessible on the internet regarding this issue, I would be mindful of the behaviors not to do in public. The only reason why the research commenced was because I wanted help. I did not know why I would sneak food and secretly eat to feel better about my internal wounds, sometimes while crying. Yet, I continued to find ways to stuff my face in private. There was always a plan in place, or a new strategy being made. I still find myself trying not to emotionally eat every so often, but this area of my life has improved tremendously.

I was never diagnosed with depression or an eating disorder, but it was an issue I carried into my college years. I was very aware that I had a problem. I dealt with this in silence because whenever I opened my mouth to talk about it, they would say "you're not depressed" or the conversation would awkwardly change to a new topic. It does something to you when you share information with someone you thought you could trust, so intimate and personal, and your words are dismissed, made to be invalid. My response in return to theirs would be silence. This was not the last issue I was silent about.

Who taught you to hate yourself?
To hate your skin
To hate your body
That you are not enough –
Why do you care what others say?

Can you tell me who I am?
You seem to know better than I do,
But you don't even know yourself...

He Put his hands on me. He put his hands...on me. I feel so betrayed.

Shhh

We walked up the stairs and silently walked into the dark room. Sounds of the city crept through the window as he closed the door behind him. All I could see was his silhouette in the moonlight. I looked around searching for a light switch. Nowhere to be found. In silence we stood, face to face. Walls never seemed to be so closed in before.

He walked towards me and tapped my arm. Backing up, I gave him the look of, "Oh, you wanna play?" So I snuck in a small tap and we began to "play fight" as we did every so often, but this time he began to get a little more aggressive. "Ow! That hurt!" I said. That seemed to be an invitation for him to hit me harder. His hands, soft and gentle, made their way to my pants with no hesitation and tried to unbutton them. Nervously I laughed and said no. See, this was weird. This was my friend, and here I was, in this beyond-awkward situation. His hands moved and he began to rough house me again. I told him that I did not want to do this anymore. As if he did not hear me, he continued.

The hitting became more than what I wanted to be involved in and too much for my comfort. The game that we once played for fun was now making me feel very uncomfortable and alarmed. Those hands, sly and silent, found their way to my pants again, reaching for the button as he tossed me onto the bed. "Take your pants off," he said. I put my hands securely on my pants and said no. This time with a little more authority. He leaned forward against my body and kissed my lips while pinning both my arms to the bed. His locs fell over my face and his lips swallowed mine, causing whatever sounds that tried to escape to be muffled. Kissing me more aggressively now, I screamed, "NO!" I will not let this happen, I thought to myself. Kicking my legs into the air, I made an effort to hurt him, but it was a detriment to me. He sat on my legs so I would keep still. Aiming for that "prize" once more, he managed to unfasten my pants.

No words. All you could hear was the heavy breathing along with the despairing attempt to escape. I had to think fast! What to do? My arms and legs were pinned. I used my pelvic area to thrust him slightly upwards and move my legs, but it was not enough. I was not enough. With my legs spread slightly apart, he attempted to pull my pants down and failed. "Get off me!" Louder but still quiet. I was so afraid. With numerous failed attempts of pulling my pants off, he began to hit me on my arms and legs, while kissing me in-between. I was hit as if I was a burglar on the street, or as if we had never had a meaningful conversation.

The pain was bad, but it did not compare to how dead I was becoming inside. It was starting to get to me. Self-pity, self-doubt, defeated. I fell weak and he had his way. They were off. The only layer of security I fought so hard to keep was ripped off my body, my legs bare and sore from the hitting. For me the fight was not over. I looked down at my legs and pressed them together as tightly as I could, while trying to get up at the same time.

In the midst of this, I realized my disadvantage of rough housing with him. Over time, it was my weakness that was shown. He knew what I was capable of and I did not have anything extra up my sleeves. I never imagined that he had the strength that he is revealing now. Compared to his, my arms were not strong enough to keep him off me. He pulled my legs apart as if he were ripping the legs off a rag doll. Exposed, my heart felt as if it would jump out of my chest. The walls were closing in on me by the second. Everything was happening so fast. As he came closer to inserting himself into me, I tried once more to escape, but it was too late. It was already happening. He put himself inside of me with so much force. With each thrust, a piece of my soul died. Silent tears streamed down my face as I lay on the bed of shame, while my heart screamed to be rescued. Wishing I would have given notice to the signs so it would have never happened. Wishing I was not so naive.

He noticed my tears, stood up, and walked towards the window. This time I did not see his silhouette, for I looked the opposite way. Numb. I felt nothing. No more tears. No more sadness. Nothing. A few minutes of silence rolled by as my soul passed on into another realm. The silence broke. "What made you do it?" I asked him in a slightly low and monotone voice. He replied, "I don't know." This time around, my question was not "why me?" It was "why him?" and "what caused him to do it?" Out of all the people I did not know, why someone that I trusted? He apologized. For what? What was done was done. How many more pieces of myself can I afford to have taken away? The little bit of sanity and life I had left would now be gone for a very long time, if not forever.

Ashamed, then dissociated, I stood up to look out the window. I looked for what else may be waiting for me in this world, by the dumpster, or behind a building. Whatever it was, I did not care. After staring out into the night, I walked down the stairs, said bye to his cousin, grabbed my things and walked out the door. I was embarrassed and said nothing. This scene felt familiar.

Me and a classmate had just finished a choir concert, in the seventh grade. With it being dark, we rode the public bus together, since we lived in the same neighborhood. We stopped by his house first because it was closer and he wanted to get out of his uniform before he walked me home. He invited me in and we walked upstairs after greeting his dad. I can't believe his dad let me come upstairs with his son. He took his shirt off and put on a basic tee then turned his game system on. Awkward. I just stood there waiting to leave. Seeing that we were not going anywhere, he told me to sit next to him. I sat on the corner of the bed. After a few minutes passed by, we started talking but I still was not comfortable.

He stood in my face and tried to force me to give him oral sex. He pushed me over and sat on my chest and put his private area in my face. I kept my lips tightly sealed. He put his hands on my face, trying to force my mouth open. Too disgusting to bite, I found another way to get up. I do not remember all of the details. However, I recall myself feeling angry and embarrassed. I remember him standing against his wall and pulling me close to him, after I started to cry, to tell me that he was sorry. He kissed my face. Going downstairs his dad said, "What? Her hair is not messed up?" I just walked down the stairs out of the door. What an example of a father.

This time I was 18 and the situation was not far off from my middle school encounter. He followed behind me, failing to make conversation as we made our way to the bus stop – trying to silence his conscience. I did not reciprocate the effort. Nothing in my mind mattered at that point, and nothing seemed to make sense to me. The bus that I needed to ride home was approaching. He leaned towards me and gave me one final kiss, setting ablaze the last thread of life.

I stepped onto the bus and paid my fare. As the bus drove off, I did not turn back to see him, not once. Making my way through the aisle of the bus made me feel as though I was walking towards my death sentence and the passengers were the witnesses. Their eyes pierced my heart like they knew what just happened, or maybe they saw me as a jezebel because it is night and there was a guy at the bus stop. All the attention seemed to be on me. I sat in the seat towards the back and stared into the darkness for the rest of the ride home, leaving behind what was done in the dark. When I arrived home, about fifteen minutes later, I adjusted my voice and said hey to everyone in the room, pretending that things were okay. My automatic smile was plastered on my face long enough to make it upstairs without being questioned. I did not shower immediately. My mom would have been suspicious if I did. After a twenty-minute wait in my room, I finally headed to the bathroom and took a shower, watching the droplets roll off my dirty body. After that night, I never saw him again. I thought about him though.

The next day I went to school. Everything was a roller coaster from there. I was too good at disguising things, pretending. My assignments from school, I still managed to complete it, but I was mentally checked out. A few more months of school left and I could move on in silence. Though, one particular night I fell to a new low. I had sex because I was afraid to say no the opportunity. It is not like anyone was forcing me to do anything. This was the total opposite of what I wanted. I messed up once again. Why didn't I just take myself home when I had the chance? Afraid of getting in too late and getting in trouble. The consequence of that decision was exaggerated in my mind. "Why can I not do anything right?!" I ended up not going back home until after four in the morning. Before I walked home that hour, I sat in a random car and cried. My tears were all over the steering wheel, face ugly. "Why?!" "I should have just gone home." I felt so dirty. If I knew what I know now, I never would have stayed. I would have never stepped foot into that house and I would have gone straight home after I got off work.

After I was raped by my "friend," I wanted the next time to be my choice. It will happen because I let it. But I truthfully did not want that either. I wanted to convince myself that I would have control over the situation, so I believed. The truth was, I was disgusted with myself. It was bad because I was totally out of character. In the midst of it all, I was a scared little girl. Even at eighteen. I was by myself at home and outside of the home. Hitting this age mark did not make me an adult.

At the time, I still had unresolved feelings and issues from when I was younger, issues from a month ago, a week ago, and yesterday. How could I possibly keep moving forward with this baggage? I had to fight for myself. No one knew what I was going through. If I tried talking about it, it was dismissed with silence. I did not grab anyone's attention until I showed my anger. Me getting good grades year after year did not do it. Some days, I could either go home and deal with what was going on there, possibly get into a fight or argument with my step-dad, or find something else to do. Everything was my fault. Someone ate the last two pieces of bread. I'm cooking too much. I am the reason why my mom and step dad are arguing. I make too much noise when I'm exercising on the squeaky floor. I am this, and I am that. I was feeling the heat of everything I was holding in. I wanted help. What would be the point of telling someone what happened to me? I figured no one would believe it, especially since I already began to put dirt on my own name. The teachers at school were worse than the students. A teacher who once said she wanted her daughter to be like me, cut her eyes at me and never spoke to me again, once she heard the news. I was filthy in everyone's eyes. No one to turn to, not even myself. Fortunately for me, it was my final year in high school.

Father,

I keep messing up. I am trying to live right but I give in to temptation whenever it is in my face. I do not know what to do.

What's Your Reality?

There is always a person created and randomly placed in someone's life to ask, "Where do you see yourself in five years?" "Ten years?" It was easy to answer when I was in high school. "I want to go to college and earn my degree in sociology. Then I want to be well established into my career." A simple, yet vague response. My deeper desire was to own my own record label or something to do with music, dance, or writing - the arts. After talking with some adults, I thought it would be more practical and socially acceptable to have a career that made sense. The pay sure didn't make sense, but I thought my heart would make up for the money I would not make.

"How will you make money by going to school for music?" Though I knew I was the bomb (over exaggerating here) at my craft, I did not have the confidence to pursue my dream, or rebuttal the opinion of others. I sometimes asked questions, to get reassurance, when I already knew what I wanted. I just wanted support. Their responses had me thinking: either I was dreaming too big, or many adults had dull and unfulfilling lives.

The question was asked again when a couple years had passed and I was an undergrad. "In five years, I will have graduated from college, successfully established in my career, with great wealth and assets. Five years from then, I will be happily married." The fact of time continuously moving forward started to sink into my consciousness. Four years had passed and I was nowhere near where I wanted to be. All I knew was the educational institution. I enjoyed my courses, doing research papers and presentations, but outside of the classroom, I believed I had nothing more to offer. During my college years, I met a few "professional students." That was not what I wanted for myself.

My goals were truly empty. The only thing that filled them was the false success narrative that had been carried for years. Make good grades, go to college, graduate from college, buy a house, get married and your life will be fabulous. Lies, lies, lies. If this were the case I would be well-off. The more time I invested in the educational institution, the more dumb I felt. That was my only investment and I became disconnected from my truth on the inside.

Time did not stop simply because I could not clearly identify my goals. Oddly enough, it seemed to go by faster. Unfortunately, I was not clear of the direction I wanted to go and my goals were extremely vague. I was getting older and going nowhere swiftly. I could feel the pressure.

Stepping onto my first college campus would test how I would establish myself. I felt very alone. Although I chose to go to a university in another state, without any family or friends, I did not expect it to be this severe. It was planned as being the cliché "new start" for me.

There was no stopping me from leaving home once I completed high school. Of course, I was like many other teens who wanted to free themselves from their parent's rules, but I also wanted to escape the trauma and negativity.

Walking around campus was weird for me, especially since I arrived a few days early. I barely saw anyone that looked like myself, and when I did, everyone had already known each other. I did not know how to squeeze myself into the mix. I have always been somewhat of a loner, so I continued to do what I knew best.

When it was not too hot outside, I would sit on the side of a walkway ramp. The least I could do was look cute while I mind my business. I had to find a focal point because every time I looked at my surroundings, it looked and felt as if I did not have anyone. Who wants to look like they do not belong? Not me. Not having any friends to start off with made me weary of my long rehearsed goals. Thankfully this did not last long at all.

There was no doubt that I would continue with my education, yet I faced the fact that I was not going to find my husband here. There was not many heterosexual men available at the time I was looking. Dang. How did my main priority change from going to a university to earn my degree to going to a university to bag a man? Before I arrived on campus, I read a good amount of articles, and how to find a husband in college was the main topic. I probably should have done more research because I was getting rookie results. There was no one pursuing me in a marriage manner.

It did not take long to build relationships, or get a boyfriend. Not one bone in me told me to enter this relationship, but I told myself, "Why not?" To keep you sane, I will share the brief version of how I opened up some gates that should have never been opened. Though I battled with my own depression on and off, I had to help my boyfriend at the time, through his episodes as well. He smoked weed as a coping mechanism. One day I decided to join him, after our date night. Did I know what I was doing? No, but he showed me how to use a bong. It was super easy, but I did not feel anything. I had no idea I was high until he turned on the game system and Mario's face appeared. He stretched his face out of proportion on the start screen and I bursted with laughter. Tears came to my eyes and I crawled to the bathroom so I would not pee myself. I could not stop laughing. I got irritated. It was uncontrollable.

I came back into the room and he was still on the start screen. His high was not as severe as mine because he had built a tolerance. Afterwhile, I wanted to jump out of the window in moving traffic. When I explained this to him later, he told me this was not normal and the batch was probably laced. Knowing this was not my normal way of thinking, I really tried fighting this feeling. On the inside, I literally talked to myself, telling my high self what to do and what not to do. "Stay away from the window."

I clinged to him. I was going through different phases. I wanted to relax and sleep, but it was like my body could not breathe and sleep simultaneously. Afraid, I told my then boyfriend to make sure I did not close my eyes. Some moments I would "pass out" mid sentence and stop breathing. He was terrified and called his friends into the room. His friend's girlfriend held me in her arms and comforted me. I cried and was so embarrassed. She stayed with me until my head was clear. The next morning I woke up high, but was sure to take myself to my 8 am class, looking like a bug eyed fool on the front row.

As time progressed, I saw how weed affected him. He became very lazy, he had more episodes of depression, and he was failing his classes. He also began to gain weight. In fact, we gained weight together. I did not like this new lifestyle I had adopted. After he was on his first academic probation, I wanted to be sure that he was in good standing again. We worked together for homework and study time. He still smoked, but he had brought his grades up enough to have his probation released. Maybe the depression was the cause of laziness and not the weed. In doing all of this, I later learned that he had kissed another girl. Where did he even find the time to do this?

As we were in our second semester of the first year, I observed a familiar trend with him. He was smoking excessively, gaining weight, cussing like a sailor, and spending money on fast food and junk food daily. Once again, he was on academic probation and he did not tell me about his failing grades until it caught up to him.

He and I had a shared friend. This friend came to me one evening and blatantly told me that I was being cheated on. I thanked him for letting me know and waited before I entered confrontation mode. When my boyfriend was in sight, I asked him if he had cheated and he said yes. I wish the truth had come out that easy, but he initially lied. I was frank and told him that I was informed. I also said we can call her right now and ask together. He confessed. I felt my fist ball up. I was angry and silent. So I left him standing in my room. How could he be so insecure and worried that I am talking to so many guys, then pull something like this? I wish I would have left the first time. Instead, I just wrote about the conversation we had:

"Ugh... I want to be by myself right now, not necessarily not having anyone in my corner, but I want to just think about me right now.

Last night he said that he thought I was talking to another guy again. It has always been just him. Since then I've just been thinking about how things were earlier with us. How he didn't invite me anywhere when he and the others would go out, when he would hurry and let go of my hand when he would see other girls or he would hear someone coming, how he got so upset when he and Ashley couldn't hang out one night... of course I have the thought that maybe I was here for his personal needs, to make him feel good. And I was dumb enough to stay. I remember him telling me that he loved me even before he knew me, yet he cheated on me. Today he still has doubts about me, jealous of others. How can I say I love someone when my heart is constantly going through a whirl? And honestly, I think that if he and Ashley would have hung out that night, then he would have cheated on me again if he hadn't already. I just feel so many things right now :'(. I feel like I don't have anyone I can give my all to. That I can't talk about things without being judged. I told him something about my past and he said he didn't even want to touch me or mess around anymore :'(. I feel so many things right now. What am I still doing here? I care about him a lot, but what about me and my heart? And I know that a lot of this is my fault because I stayed and let it continue to happen. He keeps saying can you show me that you love me more. It would come through naturally if we weren't constantly going through the same thing. I just told him the day before that I thought I was gradually falling in love with him.

And it wasn't easy for me to say that either. What more does he want from me? And now that he has brought up the same thing, once again, my heart has been drawn back. I need to know that I am secure where I am, without any doubts or shakiness. I feel like I may be in a trap that is hard to get out of....well, maybe not hard. I can get out but it would be a challenge for me to stay out.
I just feel so sad.

> *How many more of these I am going to write before things get too out of hand?"*

I keep replaying my responses to the questions in my mind, 'I want to get married!" Now the response is, 'I do not want to get married." But I want to be loved and have a family. 'I want to get married and have two kids, a boy and a girl." I got 'played" and forgotten by someone who told me they loved me just about every day, for someone else whom they said they did not really care for. My supposed man was basically claimed as the man of someone else. No more questions please.

I was stuck on stupid, and it felt like the entire world was passing me by as I watched. I am still unsure of the answers I truly want to speak aloud, but I am taking it one day at a time as I slowly and crazily attempt to put my life back together. My distractions are becoming minimal. The more I hone in on my thoughts and be real with myself, the more I am willing to strip myself of assumptions and lies, including those I told myself. It all needs to go. I need to strip down to the naked truth. Strip down to me, whoever that is. Regardless of what she looks like, I am ready to embark on this journey to find her. She is worth the fight, she is worth the search, she is worth the healing, the truth, and the love. She is worthy of being whole. I am desperate for change.

I have let everyone in. Everyone! Now my guard is up and my standards are down. Sounds like an oxymoron, right? That is how I feel. Why set expectations while feeling so low? Yet, I cannot continue to pretend that I am the woman who believes that being sexually active with whoever, wherever is the way I should be. It is true. God gave us the power to choose. I have been down this path with no success and with a great loss of self. Though I did what I wanted, sometimes when I wanted, I would often feel convicted. Sometimes I would cry during sex (which may have been caused by trauma) and not always know why. Through my hard-headedness, I had to practice applying the knowledge, "My body is not my own." It is a vessel and it should be treated as such. It should not be disrespected. I was not directly taught how to do this.

People do their best to teach you what they believe is best for you, but it only goes as far as what they know. It is up to you to gain knowledge and apply it the rest of the way. You cannot allow yourself to be held back by your past.

Somewhere down the road, some of us learn how to be victims. Yes, learn. We were not simply born with the mindset that we would be someone's or some thing's victim.

This is a state of mind that is learned. For example, have you ever seen someone who you considered unattractive, yet, that person thought they were the bomb? Amazingly beautiful? Why? Because even if they had to tell themselves that they were beautiful more than one hundred times, they heard it so much to the point it was received and internalized. They now live and breathe that perception of themselves. Why couldn't I do the same? It was difficult to think that anyone besides my mom saw me as beautiful. Do I think I am beautiful? How did I get so low? How did I become this woman, this person?

I was not always ready to face myself. I have learned to play the blame game, running from accountability. I blamed failed relationships for my unhappiness, surfaced bitterness, and others for not seeing and understanding me. Though I may have believed that almost all of my problems were caused by others, I failed to look at myself. I painted myself as the victim. At the time, I was unaware of my state of mind. I was sick.

Homecoming

So much for getting out of Ohio. I would have stayed in Missouri if my scholarships came through when they were supposed to. Now what? I would miss the friends that I eventually made while there. My first year and a half of the college experience was changed for the better because of them, and my own efforts of course.

Being home felt weird. I don't even know anyone here anymore. At least that is what it felt like. The friends that I actually talked to were out of state and in other cities. Staying out late until three in the morning was not even a thought. Truth is, I mostly stayed up past midnight to do homework, study, or to work a shift as a desk attendant. My friends had to drag me out to have fun, and I regretted it when that 3 o'clock morning shift came, with an 8 am class to follow I was no longer working two jobs, the food choices were not broad and accessible, there was not a gym that I could walk to in less than five minutes, and I could not have my friends over. It was less freedom, and I did not like it one bit.

After nourishing my voice while away and gaining confidence, that all seemed to gradually dwindle away when I moved back home. I had to be quiet while at home. I did not feel comfortable being myself. I may sound like a brat, but I could barely listen to my music without headphones, or dance around in my room without being questioned, simply because my floor squeaked.

I eventually became adapted to the situation and found a rhythm that worked well for everyone, I assumed. I went for walks and exercised at parks early in the morning. I turned my music up while the headphones were on (sometimes without them) so it could fill my world. I bought my own food, most times, and utilized the kitchen when it was not being used, as I typically did. Things were more tolerable. I was eating better, and I looked good. I had control over what I wanted to do.

My mind was at ease. Eating from my mom's garden greatly contributed to that. Though there were agitating moments, I was happy to be home with my family.

I was downtown one day, going who knows where, and saw a familiar face. It was an old buddy I met when I was seventeen, when I had first moved to the city. Let's call him Tay. He seemed like a really cool guy at the time. At some point, we exchanged information and contacted one another every so often. After going off to college, I barely heard from him. Emails were sent sporadically and the efforts became futile. When he sent me a message, I would respond, then he would never write back. He would then send another email, "What's up." I would respond and there was no reciprocation. This happened more than a few times.

I left it alone, but asked about it when I saw him years later. He told me that his girlfriend at the time had gotten access to all of his accounts and was messaging all of his female friends. This should have been a red flag but it did not cross my mind as such.

Any who, I was super happy to see him again! He slimmed down a lot since last winter. Last time he looked like a bear. Instead of him walking towards me, this time we walked towards each other. "Heyyyy." I know I was cheesing when he said that. I would not have been surprised if I started skipping towards him. He gave me a big hug. We talked for a little bit and he asked me what bus I was getting on. I told him the number 7.

Once my bus came, he jumped on with me. Usually, he would ride the bus with me for about 2 stops then get off. We actually chilled for the remainder of the day. I remember us walking around under the hot sun like tanning was a thing for us. Shoot I did not care. I had my friend back. We went to a park and I felt like a kid again.

Tay is the first person I have interacted with, outside of normal stranger talk, since I have come back home. As he walked in front of me, I jumped on his back. Thankfully he caught me because he had no idea I was coming. I had missed him. And it felt good to be with someone familiar. After I was done trying to beat him up and what not, he led me towards a bench to sit down and we listened to music. We both shared music from our ipod and mp3 devices. I decided to let him listen to the songs I wrote and recorded myself. Surprisingly he liked it. Out the blue, he sees one of his friends. He introduced us and they both put their cents in on how they met. The guy seemed funny. He was not loud, was not disrespectful, and he was clean. He was cool in my book. I can see why they were cool. He said, "Y'all know what? Y'all are going to get married." I denied that so quickly. I was not feeling that at all. "We're just friends," I said. I noticed a slight change in Tay's face but did not pay it too much mind. I just needed everyone to know that Tay and I were not in a romantic or exclusive relationship. Friends is what we were and that is how it will stay. Nothing more.

After a while, his friend had to leave. We left about thirty minutes after him. We randomly decided to go to a studio on campus, where someone was working on a song. He was an aspiring rapper and his girl was going to school there, OSU (Ohio State University). Tay knew him. He said that he was supposed to work on a song with him but he never did it. Today was the day. The guy gave him the words to sing, but Tay was having a hard time. I stepped in and gave him a few variations of how he could get the job done. Just like that, I was asked to help the crew with other projects. I accepted. From then on, we all were together a lot – me, Tay, the rapper, and his girlfriend.

One night we all went to a hotel with two beds. You should already know the arrangement. Though moments like this made me nervous, I tried my best to never display that, especially if everyone else was unbothered. This was new for me. Though I had a boyfriend in college and he was in my dorm room each day, this felt completely different. Since the other two were a couple, I felt as if the situation called for us to pretend that we were a couple as well, but I did not want to do that.

Tay and I were up talking for hours, with the same excitement little kids hold when they read books under the covers with a flashlight. I enjoyed talking with him. Out of nowhere he pressed his lips to mine and kissed them. I instantly melted. It was not a kiss that took my breath away, but it was spontaneous. Definitely a surprise to me. I did not say anything or try to stop him. For a second I thought about the two people who shared a room with us. Are we trashy? Probably. This was not lady-like, but for reasons that did not matter, I still said nothing. I slowly pulled back, not so into the moment as I previously was. He pulled me closer and we kissed more. Was I acting out of nervousness? Was this my rebound moment? It has only been about four months since my last relationship, and for a long time he was all I could think about or speak of. Not sure if this is the case, but I was rolling with it. He also started to move quickly once I told him about someone who wanted to make me his girl. That never went anywhere because of this random detour.

For some reason, this did not feel strange at all. I was kissing my friend, I had convinced myself. My stranger friend. He tried taking it further and my eyes got big, even in the dark. I was not feeling that. I moved his hands away. We kept kissing and he tried again. His hands were pushed away again. 'I'm on my period." That was the end of it. I see I have a difficult time saying no. Yet, I allowed the act to continue for weeks. We were becoming a 'thing."

Watch the company you keep and who you choose to be involved with. One decision, one yes, can impact your entire life.

Finally Yours

I seriously did not see this coming. How did this even happen? One day you are barely more than a stranger who has my number, next we are in some sort of relationship. Just me and you.

Oh yeah! You reminded me of how I have known you for all of this time, gave everyone else a chance, but never gave you one. First, who is everyone? You do not see how many people I turn away. I am not pressed. Two, I just did not see you as more than a friend, yet again, here we are crossing boundaries that are beyond the friend zone.

I remember now. This is exactly how it happened. We had that conversation one night across the street from my mom's house. You told me how you felt – that you wanted to be with me and you are not like the other guys who ruined their chances with me. I listened, and I was going to leave it at that and call it a night. He seemed upset as I nonchalantly walked across the street and said good night. As I was walking up the stairs to go into the house, I remembered asking my mom what she thought about me and Tay. She said, "It seems like you really like him." I laughed a little. "Me?" I do not know what she saw, but I did not feel like I liked him that much. That thought sank into my heart that night and I thought, maybe she is right. I must really like him more than I know myself. I turned around and ran to him. "Wait!" He had already started walking and was almost halfway down the next block. He stopped under the street light when I called him. We met each other halfway, then I hugged him as tight as I could. "I'll give you a chance." Before the sentence fully left my mouth, I heard a strong "NO!" A voice saying not to be with him, followed by the feeling of doom. I ignored it. I could not take back my words. That would hurt him more.

I had a boyfriend now. I have to admit, things felt a little different, but not so much. I just know that I enjoyed being around him. We were together almost every day. One particular day when we were walking around the park, about three older couples looked at us and smiled. That made Tay smile, which then made me think that maybe there is something special about us that everyone else but myself noticed. I was not certain, but I was starting to like this idea of having a friendship that can grow into forever. I got the approval from the public elders. I can move forward now. What was it that took me so long to give him a chance? It could be the on and off communication or the fact that I just was not interested, but here I was, waltzing around with Tay, slowly, slowly falling deeper into it.

Another day at the park, this time I would meet him there. You will never guess what happened next when I arrived. I saw a child walking alongside him. A child! And the child was his. One of my rules for dating was that I did not want to date someone who had any children. I was too young for that. I was not trying to be anyone's step mother. I have not even lived my own life, let alone I felt like a child myself. I did not bring this issue up immediately that day. Tay was so happy to introduce his son to me.

Mmm, I did not care how cute Tay thought his son was, we did not discuss this at any point of knowing one another, and I was not impressed with this approach. Very aware of how this could have an effect on the child, I waited until later in the day to have the discussion.

Tay swore up and down that he told me about his son. "No you did not. I would not forget about you having a child. Plus, it was one of the top 'no-nos' on my list. I did not want to date anyone who already had children." That could come with so many problems. He tried to use the saying, "we come as a packaged deal." Well, you two can be packaged somewhere else. This is not what I want and I was not made aware of this. Surprisingly, he tried to compromise so I would stay. I should have noted that as another red flag. Anyone who is willing to make a compromise over their children just so someone will be with them says a lot. Anyone who is willing to be with that person speaks volumes as well. I cannot recall what Tay's bargain was, but I do know what it was like for my mother to be a single parent. I thought about how it must have felt if someone told my mom they did not want to be with her because she had children. I stayed. I was no mother but I knew how to love and be compassionate. This was a challenge I was willing to take on.

Later that evening, Tay, his son, and myself went back to his apartment. Lo and behold when he opened the door, the child's mother was in the house. You can tell she was upset when she saw me. It was obvious that Tay did not inform her I was with him. Shoot, I was not aware that she was going to be there and had a key to his place. Initially seeing her, I did not know who she was. Either I was stupid, naïve, insecure, or all of those things and more, but I should have just called it quits after that day.

It seemed to be one thing after another. Not too long after that incident, I noticed an incoming text message in his phone from a girl asking was he coming over that night. The text came in at ten that night. He said she was just a friend, then asked me why I was going through his phone. Thinking back on things, I wish I would have just had the confidence to say, "I don't want to date you anymore," but it continued. The more we went around town together, the more I noticed how many people he knew, the more girls who knew him, and vice versa. Who are they, and why are there so many of them? What the heck did I get myself into?

I remember Tay, the rapper, his girlfriend, and myself were looking for a place to record music one day. Tay suggested that we go to a spot he knew of. When we got there, it was a house. A girl answered the door. She smiled and welcomed everyone. Her hair was short, not going past her ears, and dark. Her frame was skinny. Tay introduced everyone by name and began conversing with her shortly after. Like an idiot, I was standing, waiting for him to sit, so I could sit next to him. Eventually, I took a seat on the couch, the other two were still standing by the door, and Tay and the girl were talking and making goo-goo eyes the whole time. As if I was not there, as if I was not his girl, those two talked with close proximity to one another. I said nothing. I just watched. I later asked if there is history between the two of them, Tay said yes. Exhale. Another one. There were girls everywhere. All of whom he would say were just friends.

...Why are you settling?

You're still lying to yourself...

Life's Filler Episode

I was out of school for a semester, and I was happy to be back. Life outside of school was so boring. I still lacked friends and all I could think of was finishing my remaining two and a half years of school. Instead of going to another private school like I had planned, I made the decision to attend a community college. Is this beneath me? Of course not. I was never told about the potential value of a 2-year institution. I harbored the belief that students who barely made it through high school, or did not have many options of pursuing a higher education, attended community colleges. Truth is, I could have taken classes at a community college during my last few years of high school, or even got my general classes completed before working towards my major courses. I was not educated on these options. I would have saved myself the trouble of "borrowing" loans and letting time slip by, as I was not quite convinced what I wanted to study.

Anyhow, I did not find any courses specific to my chosen major, but the academic advisor assured me that the classes I would sign up for would count towards required credits when I transfer to a 4-year university. Instead of being registered under social work, the closest program offered was the Mental Health and Addiction (MHAD) program.

The first few classes I took focused on psychiatry, social science, communications, and arithmetic. It was not terrible at all. I did dislike having to wake up two hours early to make it to class on time. Even when I successfully got out of bed and got ready in a good amount of time, it would still not be enough to get to class early. There were days where everything was smooth. Then, everybody and their mama would get on the bus, forming a long line out the door, the bus would run late, or someone would pull out a pocket full of change from their pocket to pay their fare. As long as I got there before 8:15 am, I was safe. In spite of the challenges, I successfully made it through the first year, one more to go!

Boiling Pot

I am so unorganized. I have been unorganized since the start of the semester. I probably shouldn't take summer courses. I honestly think I need a break from school. I'm just...I don't know what is going on. I want to finish. I want to finish this year strong, but it is not working out that way. Like, what the heck is wrong with me? What is going on? I don't know. When it comes to the process of school these days, my brain feels stale, past the stage of being robotic. Class is so boring and drawn out, sitting in class for hours. Can we please do something for the hands on learners? Please?

Why is it that I cannot seem to pass this one class? Not even with a C? This is ridiculous and embarrassing. My white history course was the most boring and the most challenging. The information given just did not make any sense to me. Maybe I am stressed out and this challenge arose because the universe knows I am trying to better myself. I continued the course, but decided to drop it before it reflected on my transcript as failing. Thankfully, I had heard this information by word of mouth. The next semester, I registered for the same course with the same professor. Idiot!

It was the only time slot and day that fit my schedule, and I desperately needed to pass this class. This landed me with the same outcome – a failing grade. This time I did not wait as long to drop the course. It was obvious where it was going. I took that L and accepted the W that would later gleam on my transcript.

Why is my life crumbling when I am so close to the finish line? It is like I cannot get a break. Every time I try to do well, something else comes up. I need to speak to someone about this. Coincidentally, I discovered that an advisor from the Ohio State University would be on campus, by looking at the campus website. I met with the advisor immediately. Here is where I received the great news. I had everything I needed to make my much needed move. Finally, I had met the requirements to transfer to OSU. Silly geese. The pre-requisites have already been met. I do not believe that this information would have been shared with me otherwise. So, I am thankful for the turbulence.

Finally! I had more than enough credits and passing grades to attend The Ohio State University. Once I reviewed my degree audit at the community college and compared it to the university's course requirements, it was then that I discovered I could have applied long ago. I told Tay and he was excited for me. By this time, I was in my own apartment with my full-time job as a State Tested Nurse's Assistant.

I was kicked out/I walked out of my mom's place on Mother's Day. It stemmed from another argument with my step-dad. It was a day when he was just waiting for a pen to drop, so he could explode. It was obvious tension and I was ready for whatever. I was not sparing feelings that day. "Today is my day and I don't even care."

There has been thickness in the air with my step-dad and I for years. My mom always told me that we could talk about anything, and if the time ever came where I had sex, let her know. I told my mom about me losing my virginity on my way to school, when we were by ourselves. When I got home, not even 5 seconds in, her then, recent boyfriend, was barking at me. Asking, "How could you do that to your mother?" I was ganged up on at the door. Everyone watched, my mom and two brothers. My mom cried. I got called all types of names that day, and hit on. Did anyone step in? Yes. I did. I stood up for myself.

Fast forward to Mother's Day. The most vivid and last thing I remember before leaving was spitting on him after an argument and fight had erupted. I made sure it was a good one too. I know that it is one of the most disrespectful things someone could do. In that moment, that held more power than my fist could release. I was reckless y'all.

All of my things were left at mama's house. I was on the bus line and did not have anywhere to go. I called Tay and told him what happened. I do not believe we were on the best terms but he met me where I was. For about one to two nights we slept in his dad's car, which he was not aware of. On the third or fourth day I bought a used car. By the end of the week I had an apartment. This was not how I envisioned meeting my goals, but it happened. I had not realized that I had that much money put aside. Go me!

I was not excited or anything like that. Unfortunately, moving into my new place was not joyful, maybe because Tay was with me and it was a unit he suggested. Oddly enough, before the fight, I was looking for apartments a week prior and circled my top options, but that was all left behind. After he assisted me in bringing my belongings from my mom's house to the apartment, I was ready for him to go. Instead of verbally telling him this, I left it in my mind. Little by little, I noticed his clothes and materials being left in different parts of the apartment. Why did I not speak my mind, you may ask? Well, I felt that I owed him my silence on the matter. Though I knew he was no good for me, he helped me transition from my mom's house, from my car, to my apartment. Would it be rude to say, "Thank you for helping me. You can go now"? Maybe so, but truthfully, I did not owe him anything. At the least he could have been fine with a thank you and a God bless, don't let the door hit you on the way out. Regardless, he stayed and that was that.

Turning Tables

I did it! I am finally at the Ohio State University. I have avoided it for years because I was afraid of the size of campus. It is actually not that terrifying once you get around. For my first semester, I registered for 20 credit hours, thinking it would help me catch up to speed. It did, but it definitely involved many helping hands and restless nights. Luckily for me, I had access to the gym at the RPac, to relieve stress. I had made up in my mind that I wanted to get my healthy back.

Tay and I had exercised together on and off. He was in his off season and I was ready to start back up. I had worked up the confidence to jog around the track for at least one mile, a few days of the week, if not every day. I almost died on the first day. Oddly enough, your girl felt stronger and encouraged to do more. It did not take long for me to feel better and see results, paired with other exercises. I was feeling myself. The following week, I felt exhausted. Why was it so hard for me to make it around the track? I also noticed that my belly was a bit softer. Tay told me I must be exaggerating because he did not see anything, but I definitely saw the change, especially after being excited about tightening up. This was not the news last week. It must have been something I ate. With that, I got on the ground and did ab work. Tay stayed with me instead of going to play basketball with his boys, like he usually did. His company was appreciated. Tay was not perfect, in the least, but I can honestly say that he had grown on me, yet again.

It was not long before we got into an altercation. It was in the works. Of course I started it. I looked through Tay's phone when he was in the bathroom – a childish move. I saw a message pop up on his phone from his female friend. For the longest time, I just knew I was being lied to. I had a hunch he was involved with his female friend, for years, but I did not have proof. Let us pause here very briefly. I know someone reading this is probably saying to themself, "Years? You stayed with him for years feeling like he was cheating and you still stayed? Why!?" I was not in a healthy state of mind. I used to ask myself these things as well. Let us continue. I would ask, and he would brush it off. Tay and his friend also worked at the same place because she helped him get the job there. Though I expressed to Tay that this was an issue for me, it was dismissed as me not wanting to support him. He also brought up how difficult it has been for him to get a job with his background and record. I understood that, but he knew my feelings about the situation and counted them short. If you love me like you say you do, why can't you just choose me?

This day, I found a text message that read, "I am not coming down there just to have sex with you." It was a message years old, but I was pissed because the date reflected a time when we were active and in a relationship as well. Even in that present day, Tay would go to her house to babysit and spend the night, or eat at her place. Boy, was I stupid. It made me think of the recent night when I cooked dinner and he never came home. While he was in the bathroom, I asked him about their history. I asked him if they had ever had sex. He said no. I asked again. As he danced around the question, I calmly made my way throughout the small apartment, gathered all of his things, folded his clothes, and took my key off of his key ring.

He came out of the restroom and I asked him again. Tay asked me where this was coming from, I told him the truth. Of course he was upset that I went through his phone, and I cannot justify that it was right. He noticed his things placed in one area. Tay's response about the message was that his friend was talking about someone else, which did not make sense to me. If that were the case, the remaining messages surrounding that one were out of context.

Honestly, I was so tired of being this girl. Paranoid and looking for proof of his wrongdoing. I did not trust him, yet he was still at my place, driving my car, eating my food, asking for money to 'pay back", entering my body, with nothing else to show. I felt like spoiled goods. These issues poked their heads in the beginning of our relationship, but for some strange reason, I could never leave. I know for sure it was not the sex, but it was something deeper than that for me.

"Where were you the other night?" "What do you mean?" he replied. I asked again, "Where were you the other night? You didn't come home." "Oh, she invited me to a barbeque and I was too tired to get on the bus," he said. "I thought you two weren't talking like that anymore." "We wasn't, but then she just wanted to have a few people over." "Get out of my house." He smacked his lips, "Quit trippin'." "Get out, now!" After telling Tay to get out, he refused. He snatched the key out of my hand and it got worse from there. Soon after, we were physically fighting, and my neat little pile of clothes were thrown across the apartment floor.

Towards the end of the month, I found out I was pregnant. Shortly after that, I found out he did not pay his portion of the rent for that month, while I was away at a women's retreat. All he could say was, "My bad."

Look at what I let happen.

I find it funny that you say I am your priority...
There is nothing in between,
There is no you without me,
And the sun doesn't seem to set without us...
Yet you wait on her,
Day in
The sun rises to the routine of you waking with her
Not me
Your priority
Your queen
Supposed to be...
Your words does not fit your actions
And she seems to always be there at the end of the day.
If the sun sets with us,
How then does it rise with you two?

I was

    fragmented

  when we met

       As were you

Compensating for the lack thereof

    In things

  And Shes

   They began

       where I was not

    Adding parties

    does not

    make

     Us whole

  only more fragmented

My wings were broken
You decided to ride it
Like a surfboard
Against the wind
Between the raindrops
Then left when the water was too heavy.
They no longer served a purpose for you

Note to Self (from my past self):

Live your life on the edge. Don't be afraid to fall and make mistakes. You're not always going to get it right. I also think you should speak out more. Say what's on your mind, or else the problem may continue. You're so beautiful. Don't give up on me, okay? I need you more than you could know. You have so many things to do and your journey has barely begun. Be the person that you are meant to be. Of course it isn't going to happen over night. You're still in the process of growing. Ask God to make you whole. Have you even talked to him lately? No wonder you're falling apart. You can't go too far without him and you know that. Well, just hold on. Everything is going to be okay. Just keep your head up and don't bring yourself down. You affect yourself more than anyone else. Don't be your own worst enemy. That's the devil's job. Don't let him consume you. Remember that the battle is already won. All you have to do is stand. Stand, girl. You can do it. I know you can. Haha you just don't know how great you are going to be...the role that God has for you. (Ha) Girl...if you only knew. I'm excited for you. I can't wait until you get to that place where you are destined to be. I love you. Be strong. The battle is not yours, it's the Lord's. Take care darling.

Open Letter

It took me a long time to get to the point where I can live my life without you and be content. Well, you're not totally out of my life. We have come a long way and I cannot think of possibly getting back with you. I love you, but I cannot be your wife. I remember you proposed to me when our daughter was in the hospital. It would be a cruel joke if you were my husband to be.

I have done you wrong as well. I gave my body away, carelessly, and played with both our hearts. Please forgive me.

Every time you mentioned us being together, I felt ugliness. Whenever you said that you love me, all I can do was go against you. I did not believe you. How can you love someone so much that you make it your business to start a family with another woman, who has a child, while neglecting your own? Let alone our child was in the hospital fighting for her life, as you played games with women over the internet, because you was "bored."

I have had numerous conversations with you. Sharing my feelings about the state of our relationship, feelings of rejection and neglect, feeling unloved and unwanted. I hate that I was foolish enough to stay with you so long. I did not want to be the woman who was not strong. The woman who did not have the muscle to stay with her man when challenges arose. But I became more suspicious the more neglectful you became.

Of course it seems obvious when you cook dinner for two and only one is present to eat at the table. Or you can't make it to our planned dates because you're babysitting, you're helping someone move, you're doing this and that! What about me? Did I not deserve your attention too? I mentioned my concerns to you. You assured me, no, you told me I was trippin'. Was I? I started to feel like I was going crazy, and maybe I was creating a false story in my head. Those thoughts entangled me until I realized that you kept doing the same thing. I made the dumb decision to check your messages. I started with your email. Bam! I found proof. I asked you about the evidence I found. You confronted me about invading your privacy.

I must admit, it sucks being confronted when you are in the process of confronting someone yourself. The entire situation was flipped onto myself and my efforts were ceased. That did not stop me. What else was I to do if you were not honest with me? It was the only way I received the truth.

Bringing up the past and ways you have hurt me did not pierce you, it pierced me. I grew into bitterness and no longer knew the feeling of genuine kindness towards you. I did not know myself. I had gained weight, stopped singing, dancing, journaling, and many other things. I spent my time at home and did nothing but sit in hate that I created.

Over and over again, I would think of moments where you chose someone else over me. I gave you everything you had asked for, and everything I saw that you needed without you verbalizing it. Was I not the woman you needed? Although I reached a point of feeling like an object, I still sought your validation. I did not care if I continued to give my body to you, even if I felt more numb the more I did.

I used to write poems about you, then I would read them to you. The desperation for understanding perspired on my skin. Even then, the drops were too dry for you to see, or maybe your lenses were dirty themselves. Am I worthy now? Am I good enough? Can you see me? If I cannot satisfy even you, what use am I?

After a while, I wondered if I made sense anymore.

One more thing. Please forgive me for placing on you, burdens to heal me and set me free. You are not God and that is not your role. I am also seeking your forgiveness for enabling you and not allowing you to fall and become the man that you could be. I am not your mother.

God, can you hear this broken hearted girl?
I need you!
I don't want to be like this anymore!
I want to feel the love you have for women like me –
Those who have lived a life of sin
And gave their body away,
Who have denied you,
Who have ran away from you...
But still want you.
Can you love even me?
A mess? A storm? A work in progress?
I am desperate for you
Please hear me
I am desperate for change.

Bleeding Bitterness

"God what's wrong with me?" I know I have neglected you most of the time, but I need to talk to you now. Is God my rebound?

I am not always available...I do not always make time for the Most High God, yet his presence is there when I seek him. Acknowledging this forces me to reflect on how God must feel when I choose men over him, my job over him, social media. I thought of it this way, God expels unconditional love, grace and mercy, and he gives us the choice to live by his word – to walk with him. I chose others instead. Knowing this was not the right decision, I still did not understand why there was a pattern placed over me which allowed men to cheat on me and desire other women while being with me. It is because I did not learn my lesson during those times, so the cycles continued.

Does God's heart experience clenching pain when we reject Him? It saddened me to think of the hurt I placed on The Most High, transferring the same hurt that was done to me. Wanting someone's love, but they give it to someone else – unrequited love.

I had become very unattractive and not the best person to be around. I hid it very well. I smiled on the outside, but crumbled on the inside. It had gotten to a point where my work and relationships were being affected. I wanted help. I needed time to heal. Thankfully, the healing process commenced even before I fully committed myself to Christ Jesus.

I remember I was in my small, one bedroom apartment, crying to God in the middle of my living room floor. Not only did I hate where I lived, but I was having a depressive episode. I was pregnant and did not want to go through this, especially while carrying a child. 'God, I don't want to deal with this anymore!" I cried and cried, pouring my heart out. Then I said again, " I don't want to be depressed anymore!" It was not more than twenty minutes that had passed when I felt the heaviness of depression lifted from me. I felt a lightness. I started smiling and thanking my heavenly Father. I can honestly say that depression has not had any power over me after that moment, since the year 2016.

It took baby steps, but I was worked on in other areas as well. At the time, I believed I was completely whole because my depression had lifted. That was a major issue for me over the years, so there was nothing else that crossed my mind of being a hindrance to my healing and progression. It was not long before suppressed issues had come up. The healing of one area made room for me to be healed in all of them. This is a journey!

The feeling of rejection and low self-esteem from my childhood crept up at home, my place of work, and at church. I would exhaust myself to please others in search of acceptance. I would also make myself small in the way I walked, my intellect and the tone and volume of my voice, in an attempt to make others feel comfortable or not intimidated. Spending more time with God helped, self-reflecting, and communing with others helped me to grow into my true identity (I am still growing). I was empowered to walk away from dead people and places that were not serving me, where before I would have stayed in a place where I knew I was dying.

I can now say that I have overcome the bondage I had in many areas I have struggled with for years, including my relationship with Tay. I can sit next to him and be okay, not wanting to cry or scratch his eye balls. I can smile at him genuinely. I do not hate you.

I can now say that I love myself, and I am beautiful.

My story is still being written. At the end of the day, I am a better mother, sister, daughter, friend, and future wife, because of what I have gone through and overcome. As I get out, I am taking people with me. You are not alone in this.

Until next time...

Closing Remarks

I thank everyone who has taken the time to read my words. What you have chosen to journey on were pieces of my mind and heart. Though fragmented in areas, it is representative of where my mind was in each stage of events. Writing this has allowed me to reflect and shine light on many things I had tucked under the rug. No one needs to know about what I have gone through, right? I will tell you now, I was a little nervous telling this much, in the beginning. That is why it has taken me so long to get this small story out. I was nervous about who would be hurt by my testimony, then I realized that this is my healing and I take ownership of my experience. Was I reckless? Yes. Am I perfect? Absolutely not! Do I still make mistakes? I try to be better every day.

I just hope that someone can learn from my experience. Please do not be afraid of your beautiful voice. Be as bold as a lion, as you ought to be. Take back your authority.

Woman, man - love yourself. We live in a world that has hate in many places, but there is also love. Loving yourself is a journey in itself. Even if you have to endure it alone, take that leap towards freedom and healing.

Freedom - an awesome word. What does it feel like for you to be free? For you to no longer have chains on your heart, your mind, your body? Everything that keeps you down cannot be seen with the natural and naked eye, but you know it is there because you can feel it. And oftentimes you try to shake it because you want to make it seem as if everything is okay, but the truth is, you are bothered. You cannot be set free, until you acknowledge what is there. Until then, you will stay where you are.

Be encouraged everyone. Your story is still being written.

Year after year, a piece of my pure heart would vanish and I found myself not recognizing who I was anymore. My privacy was invaded at a young age, and there was nothing I could do about that. At least that's what I thought. If God could heal me from a wounded heart, caused by disappointment, abuse, trauma, and then some, he can do it for you. And guess what, my healing process is *still* taking place today. The process is different for everyone, be patient with yourself.

Father,

I thank you so much for loving me. I cannot believe that you were so persistent, patient, and determined with me. Your love is so strong that I was able to learn to love myself. Your love came with healing and freedom, peace and joy. I LOVE MYSELF!! And it is because of you. I can trust again. I now have love to give my daughter, my family, friends, strangers, my enemies, and my future spouse. I feel so blessed to be at this point, to now say that I am FREE.

I repent for each deed I have done to break your heart and go against your word. I still have not "arrived" to my desired destination but I am content in you. I thank you, Father, for your patience with me, for loving me when I did not love myself, my healing, and teaching me to love and trust again. I welcome you into my heart and my life, and I give you permission to take space within me and around me. You are welcome here.

For each negative thing that has been planted in your life, even before your birth: curses, sins of your father and mother, known and unknown transgressions, anything meant to destroy your future and lineage - we uproot it, and declare that it will be destroyed. We cancel the plans of the enemy right now!

You are a child of the Most High God. You are loved. You are necessary. You are worth fighting for.

What you have gone through may be painful, but you will grow through it. Weapons may have formed against you, but they shall not prosper. Words may have been sent to slay you, but it will fall onto concrete and will be made null and void.

You are victorious! You are brave! You are skillful! You know how to love. You have peace and joy! Walk in it.

"Someday, the things that held me bound will not be a distant memory, but a testimony of how I became free."

I Love You

References

Gluck, Samantha. "Eating Disorders: Common in Young Girls | HealthyPlace." Healthyplace.Com, 14 Jan. 2014, www.healthyplace.com/eating-disorders/articles/eating-diso rders-common-in-young-girls.

Scott, Jennifer R. "The Differences Between Binge Eating and Overeating." Verywell Mind, 4 June 2020, www.verywellmind.com/when-does-overeating-become-bin ge-eating-3495807.

Sol, Cleo. Why Don't You. 23 Nov. 2017.

CPSIA information can be obtained
at www.ICGtesting.com
Printed in the USA
LVHW042243310820
664669LV00002B/233